# Getting Ready for Jesus

Carolyn Byers

3

REVIEW AND HERALD® PUBLISHING ASSOCIATION
WASHINGTON, DC 20039-0555
HAGERSTOWN, MD 21740

This author assumes full responsibility for the accuracy of all facts and quotations as cited in this book.

This book was
Edited by Penny Estes Wheeler
Art direction by Linda Anderson McDonald and Stephen Hall
Cover art and illustrations by Chris Molan
Cover design by Stephen Hall
Type set: Palatino 12 pt.

PRINTED IN U.S.A.

**Library of Congress Cataloging in Publication Data**

Byers, Carolyn.
   Forever stories / Carolyn Byers.
      p.    cm.
   Summary: Retells in story fashion the life of Jesus from the age of twelve to His death.
   1. Bible stories, English—N.T. Gospels.    [1. Bible stories—N.T.]    I. Title.
BS2401.B74    1989
232.9—dc20                                           89-37757
                                                    CIP
                                                      AC

     ISBN 0-8280-0504-4

Dedication
for
Brenda, Branton, Brady,
and Brani

# Contents

# Red Doorposts

Pharaoh was an evil king who prayed to many gods. He prayed to Ra, the sun god. He prayed to Hapi, the river god. He prayed to Hathor, the cow god. He even let people worship him. He called himself Horus, the hawk-headed king-god.

Pharaoh, the king of Egypt, knew about the God of heaven. He hated Him. Pharaoh had learned about the true God from Abraham's family. God had guided Abraham's family to Egypt. They were to teach the Egyptians about Him.

Now evil Pharaoh despised Abraham's children, who were called Israelites. "The Israelites are everywhere," Pharaoh stormed. "They are like the stars of the sky. They are like the dust of the ground. We must get rid of them."

"They shall be slaves," he ordered. "Make them dig clay and gather straw. Make them make bricks. Have them plow our fields and harvest our wheat. If they won't work, beat them!"

Pharaoh set cruel bosses over the Israelites. But it seemed that the more the Israelites worked, the larger their families grew.

8

"We've got to get rid of them! Kill all their baby boys," Pharaoh said.

God saw what was happening. It hurt Him to see His children mistreated. God felt every blow given them. The Israelites were His precious sons and daughters.

The time had come for Israel to leave Egypt. God would lead them to the land of Canaan. They could live good lives there. But first God would give the Egyptians one last chance to know Him. Maybe some Egyptians would choose to join His family.

God sent Moses and Aaron, his brother, to Pharaoh. "God sent us to you," Aaron said. "God sent you a message. 'Israel is My firstborn son. Let the children of Israel go so they can serve Me. If you will not, I will kill your firstborn sons.' "

Pharaoh laughed. "Who is the Lord, that I should obey Him? Look! Our gods made us rich and happy. You are slaves. Where is your God?"

Suddenly Pharaoh did not want to get rid of his slaves. "No. No, they cannot go."

Moses and Aaron left the palace. But they would be back.

Early the next morning Moses and Aaron went to the Nile River. Pharaoh was worshiping there.

"Oh, Hapi, god of the river," they heard him say, "you are good. You are powerful. Thank you for giving us water. Without it, we could not eat or live."

Aaron spoke to the king. "The Lord has sent you a message. Our God tells you to let His people go. Because you will not obey, the river will turn to blood."

Moses hit the water with his staff. The river turned blood-red and smelled dreadful. Moses and Aaron walked away.

The river stayed red for seven days. All the fish in the river died. The people of Egypt had no clean water to drink. Only the Israelites drank clear, fresh water. Still Pharaoh would not let the Israelites leave. He wanted to keep his slaves.

11

God sent Moses and Aaron to Pharaoh again.
"If you will not let God's people leave," Aaron said,
"God will send a plague of frogs."

Pharaoh shook his head.

Aaron stretched out the staff over the river Nile. Out came
frogs—little frogs, big frogs, fat frogs, skinny frogs. There were
frogs everywhere. Everywhere except where the Israelites lived.

Now Pharaoh liked to pray to frog idols. But he did not like frogs in his bed. He didn't like frogs in his water glass or in his bath.

"I'll let the people go," Pharaoh told Moses. "Just get the frogs out of here!"

Moses prayed, and the frogs died. After the dead frogs were cleaned away, Pharaoh still would not let the children of Israel go. So God sent lice to Egypt. After lice, God sent flies. After flies came a sickness that killed many horses and cows and sheep.

Did Pharaoh let the Israelites go?

No.

How many times did God have to ask Pharaoh? What would it take for Pharaoh to listen? All of Egypt was being hurt by the plagues. Would Pharaoh's own son have to die? Would Pharaoh ever believe that God in heaven was stronger than his gods?

After the animals died, God sent boils. Then came big hailstones and lightning. The hail killed animals and people. It broke trees and flattened plants. The Egyptian countryside was in shambles. But where the Israelites lived, nothing was hurt. Maybe *now* Pharaoh would let God's people go!

Did he?

No!

After the hail came locusts. The locusts ate everything in sight. But Pharaoh still did not let the children of Israel go.

Then God turned the sky black. People could not even see their fingers. If the Egyptians wanted light, they had to go where the Israelites lived.

It was dark for three long days. That gave Pharaoh time to think. *Why didn't Ra, the sun god shine his light? Wasn't Ra as strong as Israel's God?*

*Why didn't Hapi stop the river from turning blood-red?*

*Maybe I should let Israel go*, the king thought. *Maybe I should let them go worship their God.*

After three days of darkness, what did Pharaoh say?

"No!"

What would it take to change his mind?

God didn't want to do it, but at last He sent the message. "At midnight I will go through Egypt," God said. "I will kill all the firstborn boys. But I will pass over all the houses whose doorposts are painted with blood."

Moses gave Israel exact directions. "Take a lamb and kill it. The lamb will remind you that God's Son will die for our sins.

"Put the lamb's blood on your doorposts. Cook the meat and eat it. Then be ready to leave at midnight."

Those who chose to believe God, did as He said. The oldest boys watched closely as their fathers killed the lambs. For many it was the first time they had seen a lamb die. They saw the fathers put their hands on the lambs' heads. They heard them pray:

"Dear Father, we are sorry we have disobeyed. Please forgive us. We do love You. We want to be Your children. Thank You for giving us Your Promised One.

He is like this lamb. His death brings us life. Thank You for keeping us safe. Make us good like You are.

In His name, amen.

Then the fathers dipped a hyssop branch into the lambs' blood. They painted blood on the doorposts. Then they walked under the doorposts and went inside to pack for their long trip.

Wonder filled the hearts of many sons. *Why should we do this?* It seemed so strange.

While the families were getting
ready to leave, some heard knocks on their
doors. "Who is there?" they called from inside.

"We're Egyptian friends. May we come to your house tonight?" they asked. "We know your God is strong. He takes care of you. Ra and Hapi and Hathor are not strong gods."

"Of course," came the answer. "Come in. Come in. Do you choose to worship the God of heaven too?"

"Yes, we do."

At midnight loud wails pierced the darkness. Many Egyptian men and boys died. Pharaoh's oldest son died. But inside the homes with the red-painted doorposts, no one died. Everyone was safe, even the Egyptian boys.

Pharaoh sent Moses an order. "Get out. All of you, get out! And hurry!"

# The Day Nobody Could Forget

"Jobab, you hang on to Parah's rope. Don't let her get away. Remember, this cow is afraid of barking dogs." Mother handed Parah's rope to Jobab.

"Timna, you carry your own bundle of clothes. Don't drop it. I don't know when I can wash again." Timna rubbed her eyes. Usually she was sleeping this time of night.

Jobab and Timna were just two of the thousands of children that left Egypt the night they painted the doorposts.

"Are we ready, Mother?" Jobab patted Parah's side.

"Almost. Father went to get his pay from the taskmaster. He will be back soon."

"Which road will we take?" Jobab seemed full of questions.

"I hear that we are heading toward the Red Sea. That is not the shortest way to Canaan, but it is better than going through the Philistine country. Those people would kill us for sure!" Mother adjusted her weaving frame on the donkey cart.

"Mother! Father's here. Are we ready?"

"Yes. Just as soon as I wrap up the dough. There's no time to bake it now." Mother was in such a hurry that she let the door slam behind her.

Father pointed to the sky. "Children, look at what God sent to guide us."

"It looks like a big campfire." Timna tied a knot in her bundle.

"I wonder what it will look like in the daytime," Jobab said. Parah tugged on her rope. "Easy, girl. We're about ready."

"That's right. I'm ready," Mother said. She turned to Father. "Are you ready?"

"Let's go. Goodbye, Egypt," Father said. "We're on our way to Canaan."

Not many hours passed before Jobab found the answer to his question about the big campfire.

"Timna, look. Now there is a white, fluffy cloud above us. It looks like Parah's cream."

"It's pretty. Still I like it better when its dark outside. I feel safer."

As the children walked, they had no idea that the trip would take 40 years. But God knew. He knew it would take that long for Israel to learn to shine like the stars again.

God's cloud moved with them to the sea. There God walled up the water. Jobab and Timna and all the other Israelites walked across on dry land.

God's cloud led them into the desert. Parah got thirsty and mooed for water. God knew what Parah needed, so He sent a river of water. The water flowed from a big rock.

The food Mother brought didn't last many days. When it ran out, God sent some more. Jobab and Timna found it early one morning. They brought some to their tent.

"Look, Mother! It's white and round. It tastes sweet, like honey." Timna fingered hers. "What is it?"

Mother pinched a little between her fingers. "What *is* it?" she asked.

"It's manna," Father said with a laugh. "Manna means 'what is it?' "

God's cloud led the people only as fast as Parah could walk. Steadily it moved toward Mount Sinai. There it settled on the mountaintop.

Far away from camp, Moses set up the Tent of Meeting. Jobab and Timna watched Moses go inside. They saw God's cloud move to the doorway. They knew God was talking to Moses.

"Children, God is talking to our leader," Father said. "We should pray." The family knelt in the sand beside their tent.

When Moses came out, they listened to his words. "God wants me to meet Him at the top of the mountain," Moses said. "I'm going, but I'll be back."

When Moses returned, he repeated God's words to the people.

" 'I brought you out of Egypt so you could be near Me. I want to care for you and make you happy. To do this, you need to honor and obey Me. Do you love Me?' "

Moses waited for the people to answer. In chorus, they said, "We do."

"Do you choose to obey Me?"

"We do."

God heard their reply. He was glad. He wanted to make them happy. God knew they would be the happiest if they obeyed His few rules. Those rules were so important that God decided to speak them Himself.

Once more God invited Moses up to the mountaintop. Moses came back with a message. "God is going to talk to you in three days," he said. "Wash your clothes. Take baths. Clean your tents. And pray for clean hearts. Eat simple food so you can have clear minds. God wants *everything* clean."

Then Moses told the people to build a fence around the mountain. "After it is built, do not let anything touch it," he said. "God is coming very close. This is a holy place."

The men worked together to put up the fence. The women scrubbed clothes and cleaned their tents. Everyone ate simple food and prayed.

On the third morning, lightning flashed around the mountain. Thunder followed. A thick, dark cloud moved down the mountain. The children stared. Was God *really* there? Was God so close they could almost touch Him?

*Taeeeee, Taeeeee!* A trumpet blasted the air. Timna clutched Mother's skirts. Mother edged closer to Father.

Moses invited the people, "Come near."

Jobab took a few steps forward.

"Ohhh! Look at the fire. Is the mountain going to burn up?" Jobab whispered in Father's ear.

"I don't know. Nobody has ever seen anything like this. God usually talks to men when they are alone. You are most fortunate to be here now."

*Taeeee, Taeeee!* Again the trumpet blasted. Shivers ran down Jobab's back.

"Be sure nobody crosses the fence." Moses stood by the fence to guard it.

Then the thundering stopped. The trumpet was quiet. All was silent. Even the birds stopped singing. No one spoke.

After a quiet time God spoke:

"You shall have no other gods before Me.

Do not worship idols.

Be careful how you use My name.

Remember the Sabbath day.

Honor your father and mother.

Do not kill.

Husbands and wives, love each other.

Do not steal.

Be truthful.

Do not want what belongs to others."

As God spoke, the people knelt, their heads to the sand. Some ran away. Never had they heard anything so big and powerful.

FS3-3

33

After the mountain was again still, the people came to Moses. "You talk to us. Don't let God speak, or we will die."

Moses replied, "Don't be afraid. God loves you. He just wants you to know that His rules are important."

The people shook their heads. How could they forget? They couldn't forget, they were sure.

Nevertheless, God knew they might forget. Just to be certain, God wrote out His 10 rules. He wrote them on two big stones with His own finger. He handed them to Moses to give to His people.

# Neighbors

"Jobab and Timna, listen carefully," Father said. "Moses just came back from the mountain. He brought back the stones God wrote His 10 laws on. God told Moses that He wants us to make a tent-church so He can live among us." Father moved his hands as he talked.

"God wants us to bring materials to build His church. Moses will need gold and silver. He'll need animal skins. He'll need olive oil and linen and acacia wood, too."

Father looked at Mother. "What can we give?"

"Let me think. Your taskmaster gave us earrings and bracelets. Could Moses use them?"

"Yes. I thought of that, too."

"Father," Timna said. "I have a ring. One of my friends in Egypt gave it to me. Could I give it?"

"Surely."

"And I have a silver cup I could give," Jobab said.

Mother smiled. "That's a good idea. I can spin our dried flax into thread and weave it into linen."

37

Jobab and Timna's family took their offerings to Moses for the new church. So did many other families.

"Go to Bezalel," Moses told them. "He is the building director." Bezalel told the workmen, "Put the skins here. Put the wood over there. The gold and silver can go in that tent."

Not many days passed before Bezalel sent word to Moses. "The people have brought too many things. Tell them to stop."

"We have enough," Moses told everyone. "Don't bring any more."

Everyone was interested in the new church. The children begged to see what was happening.

"Mother, may I watch the workmen today?" Jobab stood on his tiptoes.

"Yes, if you go with your father. He is gathering his tools so he can help. Remember, don't get in the way."

Jobab waited till Father was ready. Together they zigzagged between tents to where the men were working.

They found Bezalel standing by a drawing of the new church. Jobab went with his father to look.

"See, the church will have three parts. There is the court where the people can go. The front room in the tent is called the Holy Place. The priests will work there. The back room is the Most Holy Place. That is where God will be."

"What are those things inside?"

"That is the furniture. It shows us what we must do to come to God."

Father pointed to the drawing of the altar. It stood by the doorway. "When someone chooses to come to God, he goes to the altar first. He must think about the lamb.

"Then, Jobab, he goes to the washbasin and asks God to wash him clean." Father put an arm around Jobab's shoulders.

"Jobab, there is still one more thing we need to do."

"What is that?"

"We need to come to the prayer altar." Father patted his son and turned toward Bezalel.

"What can I do to help today?" Father asked.

"You may work on the wallboards. They need to be planed and sanded," Bezalel said. "The boards are over there." Bezalel hurried away to answer another worker's question.

Father lifted a plank and started to work.

During the next few months, Jobab spent many hours watching the workmen. He saw a workman melt silver dishes together. The man made a base for the wall of the Most Holy Place.

Meanwhile, Timna helped Mother spin flax strands into thread.

*Whorl-whorl-whorl*. The spindle stick danced in her hands. The spool of thread grew fat and round.

While Timna whorled, Mother wove the thread into linen cloth.

Over, under; over, under. Their hands ached. But they worked on.

"Why does Moses want so much linen?" Timna asked.

"Moses said that the outside walls will be made of linen," Mother told her.

"Why don't they use wood to make them?"

"Cloth walls are easier to fold up. That way we can take the tent-church with us when we move."

Everyone felt proud when Bezalel and his helpers brought Moses the finished pieces of the church. It looked like a big parade. They brought the ark-chest. They brought the linen curtains. They brought the high priest's robes.

Moses inspected each piece. He smiled. "It is made just like God wanted it."

Moses held out his hands over the workers. He closed his eyes and prayed. "The Lord bless you and keep you. The Lord make His face to shine upon you . . ."

On New Years's Day, Moses put the church together. He set the wallboards in their silver bases. He hung the curtains. Then he moved the ark-chest inside God's room. He opened the chest and set the ten-commandment stones inside. He placed the golden cover with the golden angels on top. He worked carefully. God would dwell there.

Then Moses went inside the priest's room. Following God's directions, he put the lamps on one side. He put the golden table on the other. He set dishes on the table and put bread in the dishes. He placed the prayer altar closest to God's room. He put incense on it.

Outside, Moses placed the washbasin just so. He moved the large altar to its spot. The people watched quietly. Moses brought a lamb to the altar. He put his hands on the lamb's head. The crowd watched and listened.

"Dear Father, we ask You to forgive us for disobeying Your laws. Thank You for giving us Your Promised One.

He is like the lamb. He will die to bring us life. We know that You can help us obey Your 10 rules. You can make us good. Please send Your Promised One soon. In His name, amen."

Last of all, Moses hung the white linen curtains around the courtyard. When he locked the last golden ring, someone pointed upward. "Look! Look up there!"

A bright cloud moved toward them.

"It's God's cloud," the people chorused.

Closer and closer it came. Larger and larger it loomed. Silently it wrapped its glory around the new church. It was so bright that even Moses backed away.

"God *is* here," Jobab whispered.

"Yes, God is here." Father spoke softly in his son's ear. "Just think, God is now our neighbor. He is just a few tents from us. Just beyond the altar and washbasin, past the candlesticks and over the curtain. There between the golden angels, God will be."

Jobab's eyes sparkled. "My silver cup is in God's room."

# Desert Boy

Zechariah placed fresh incense on the prayer altar. He lifted his hands and began to pray.

"Dear Father, I bring to You the prayers of our people. Please hear and answer them.

"We know it is time for Your Son to come from heaven . . ."

Zechariah prayed in a church. This wasn't the same one that Moses built. This temple-church was in Jerusalem, a city in the Promised Land. It was built many years later on the same mountain where Abraham and Isaac had worshiped.

For years Zechariah had studied the Bible scrolls. "A Star shall come out of Israel,"* he had read. He thought about the words. Another verse said that God's Promised One would be born in Bethlehem.** Again and again, Zechariah read the prophecies.

"I'm sure God will send Him soon," Zechariah told his wife, Elisabeth.

"I hope we see Him before we die," she said. "We are getting old."

_____
* See Numbers 24:17
** See Micah 5:2

Zechariah's turn had come to help in the Temple at Jerusalem. How Zechariah wished he had a son. Zechariah would teach him to be a priest like his father. But he had no children. He and Elisabeth had prayed for a son for many years. But no baby had come. Now they were too old. However, he still had one hope. Before he died, Zechariah hoped God would let him see the Promised One.

Zechariah stood before the prayer altar. "Please send Your Son soon," he prayed.

Suddenly he felt he was not alone. He looked up.

"An angel," he breathed.

"Don't be afraid," the angel said. "God has heard your prayers. He's giving you a surprise. Your wife will have a baby boy. You are to name him John."

Zechariah blinked. Was this real?

"John will be a special baby," the angel said. "You must feed him only healthful foods. He will help people get ready to meet God's Promised Son."

"How—how—how shall I know this is true? I am an old man."

"I am Gabriel. I came from God's throne. Because you did not believe, I will give you a sign. You will not speak until after the baby is born."

Then the angel was gone.

Zechariah turned and walked out of the Temple. He tried to speak to the people. But he could not talk.

"Mmmmmmmm. Mmmmmmmmm." No words came out.

Someone in the crowd pointed. "Look at the priest's face. It glows like a lamp."

Zechariah waved his hands. He tried to show that an angel had talked to him. The people did not understand. But they knew something important had happened.

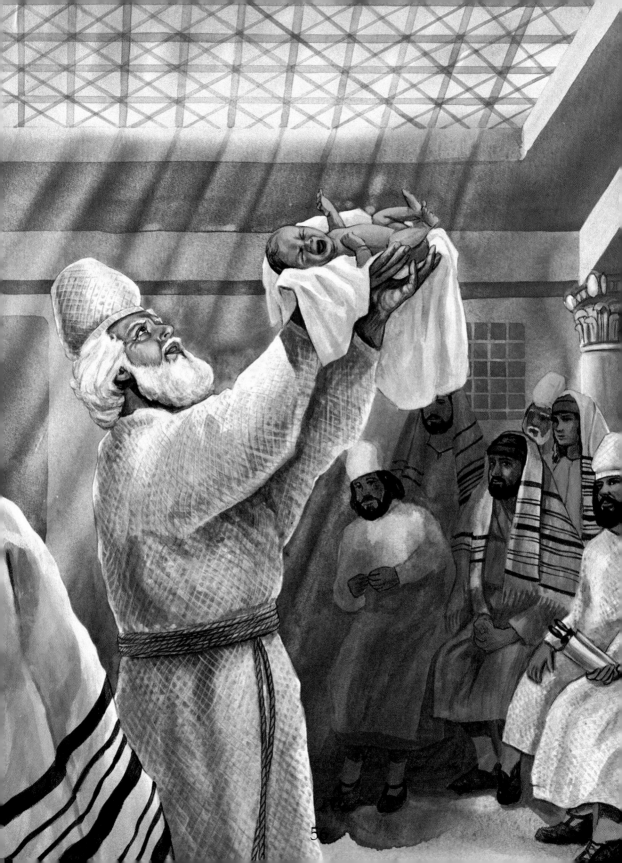

Zechariah returned to his home in the hills.

Just as the angel had said, he and his wife had a baby boy. When the baby was 8 days old, they took him to the church to name him.

"You should name him after his father," someone suggested.

"No, his name will be John," Elisabeth said.

Zechariah motioned for a writing tablet. He took a stick and wrote on the wax-covered board. "His name is John."

As Zechariah wrote, he felt something happen in his throat. He tried to speak. He could!

"Blessed be the Lord God of Israel," he cried. "This child will go before the face of the Lord to prepare His ways."*

*Luke 1:68,76

Zechariah spent many hours holding the baby. He rocked him and walked him. He cuddled him and comforted him. When John was still tiny, Zechariah told Elisabeth, "We need to move."

"Why, I like our home."

"These neighbor children will not be good for John. They will teach him bad habits."

"Where should we go?"

"I think we should move to the desert. It will be quiet there. And John can make friends with the desert creatures."

Zechariah and Elisabeth moved to the desert. Little John enjoyed digging paths in the rocky ground. He chased lizards. He found pretty stones. Elisabeth fed John good foods. She gave him fruits and vegetables. She gave him nuts and hearty bread with honey on it. She wanted John to be strong and be able to think well.

Before John could talk, Zechariah read the Bible scrolls to him. He read, "A Star shall come out of Israel."

"For unto us a child is born, to us a Son is given . . . and His name will be called Wonderful . . . Mighty God . . . Prince of Peace."*

When John learned to read, he took his father's scrolls and studied them for himself. Over and over he read the verses about God's Son. While he was still young, he felt sure that it was time for God to send His Baby.

———
*See Isaiah 9:6 RSV, Numbers 24:17

61

"People must know this," he said. "They must get ready. The Promised One is coming soon!"

John was thrilled. "The Promised One is coming," he told his friends. "We must get ready."

The news spread. People grew excited. John's friends told their friends, and *they* came to talk to John. They listened when he preached.

"Repent. Be sorry for your sins," John told them. "Show God that you want a clean heart by being baptized. Get ready to meet the Promised One."

Great crowds came to hear John. Many chose to follow God and were baptized. So many came that people asked John, "Are *you* the Promised One?"

"No, I'm not the Promised One," he told them. "I am not even good enough to untie His shoes."

The people wondered, "Who is it that will come?"